Go Figure!

102 Math Word Problems
Based On Actual News Stories

by Max W. Fischer

Incentive Publications, Inc.
Nashville, Tennessee

Cover by Geoffrey Brittingham
Edited by Jill Norris
Copy Edited by Stephanie McGuirk
Math Editor J. Noel Frietas

ISBN 978-0-86530-418-5

2   3   4   5   6   7   8   9   10   10   09

PRINTED IN THE UNITED STATES OF AMERICA
www.incentivepublications.com

Introduction

Combine the standards of the National Council of Teachers of Mathematics with middle school students' innate curiosity about the oddities of life and you get the motivating word problems in *Go Figure!* This book gives students important practice in solving word problems using a variety of problem-solving strategies. The problems can be used by individuals or in classrooms to augment math instruction, as an opening (or closing) bell ringer activity, as a sponge activity, or as an extra credit assignment.

Review the step-by-step problem-solving regimen on page four and model its use as you and your students solve the first problems together. The regimen is printed as a helpful reminder at the top of each problem. Don't forget to also review and demonstrate the different strategies that successful problem solvers use. The 102 problems in *Go Figure!* are the perfect vehicle for establishing a problem-solving regimen and introducing and practicing problem-solving strategies.

The NCTM standards call for students to have experience with a variety of problem-solving strategies. This resource book offers practice with nine specific strategies and, in addition, addresses ten distinct mathematical strands. You will also find a set of higher-order thinking problems designated as Mental Mazes.

Since the problems in *Go Figure!* are based on news stories from around the world, each problem has an obvious geographic element. Teachers may choose to have students locate the setting of each problem before the actual problem solving begins. Determining the geographic location of the new story can be easily intertwined with the preview regimen for each problem.

TABLE OF CONTENTS

The Problem-Solving Regimen

Preview: Students skim the problem to locate the basics. *Who is involved? What has occurred? What basic mathematical question is being asked?*

Read: Once an overview has been made, students now must read to determine exactly what the mathematical problem is. At this point students should be encouraged to tackle the problem as a reading problem. They should specify what question is being asked. They should make a bulleted list or web of the information needed to solve the problem.

Strategy Selection: Students should select a strategy that they think will work. *Does this problem give any hint of what strategy should be used? Have you worked a similar problem in the past? If so, what strategy did you use?*

Solve: Use the selected strategy and solve the problem. If it doesn't lead to a reasonable answer, perhaps a different one will make sense.

Review: Reread the problem. *Does the answer address the problem's question? Does it make sense? Is it given in the units asked for within the problem?*

Problem-Solving Strategies

Compute or Simplify
In many instances, the mere application of mathematical rules is all that needs to be done.

Use a Formula
Formulas are useful tools to help determine solutions in problems involving some form of measurement—geometry, temperature, velocity, volume, area, weight, distance, etc.

Make a Picture/Draw a Diagram
Some problems require that students make a picture or diagram in order to better visualize the nature of the problem. This is often true of geometric problems. The diagrams need not be overly neat, just clear enough to allow a workable model for the solution.

Make a Table, List, or Chart
A table, list, or chart can organize data needed to solve a problem by giving the information a defined order. A table can track data and help find missing data. A list helps arrange thinking about a problem.

Guess and Check

When large numbers, or a great deal of numbers, are present in a problem and only one possible type of solution is allowable, trial and error is often the best method. It allows the range of answers to be gradually lessened until the most acceptable one is located.

Find a Pattern

A systematic repetition of numbers, a pattern is useful to determine solutions for some problems. Often a pattern is presented within the problem, and the sequence becomes obvious.

Brainstorm

Brainstorming calls for creative thinking for problematic situations not previously encountered. Often done in concert with others, brainstorming permits no initial idea to be vanquished. Flexibility of thought is at a premium in brainstorming. Only with logical thinking can ideas can be dismissed, one at a time, as they prove ineffective solutions.

Work Backwards

For some problems with a string of data requiring calculations, it is best to begin with the last piece of information given.

Use Logical Reasoning

While every problem has logic to it, some are truly defined by conditions presented in the problem. Each step in the solution is predicated by logical inference.

STRATEGY USED	PROBLEM NUMBER
Compute or Simplify	1, 2, 3, 4, 6, 7, 8, 9, 10, 11, 12, 13, 14, 15, 16, 17, 18, 19, 20, 21, 22, 23, 24, 25, 26, 27, 28, 29, 30, 33, 34, 38, 39, 41, 48, 49, 50, 52, 53, 54, 56, 57, 59, 60, 61, 73, 78, 87, 88, 89, 90, 91, 95
Use a Formula	63, 64, 65, 68, 69, 71, 72, 74, 75, 76, 77, 79, 80, 81, 82, 83, 84, 85, 86
Make a Picture/Diagram	1, 62, 63, 64, 65, 66, 68, 71, 83, 84, 86, 97, 102, 104, 106
Make a Table, List, Chart	5, 16, 17, 18, 20, 32, 43, 44, 45, 53, 58, 62, 68, 92
Guess and Check	5, 14, 15, 16, 18, 20, 40, 62, 82, 94, 95
Find a Pattern	31, 33, 36, 41, 43, 44, 45
Brainstorm	41, 66, 76, 96, 99, 100, 101, 102, 105, 106
Work Backwards	13, 37, 46, 47, 51, 53, 55, 61
Use Logical Reasoning	1, 35, 36, 37, 40, 43, 51, 92, 93, 94, 95, 98, 99, 103, 105, 106

Horrible Herring

Several European airlines have banned the carrying of one of Sweden's most traditional of foods—fermented herring. They claim the cans of fish could explode, causing a bomb-like hazard in mid-air. Some Swedish people are very upset that their favorite food is being singled out in such a manner; however, while many love the canned fish, others believe the fish smells like rotting garbage as it ferments—or bacterially breaks down—in the sealed can. The herring lovers explain that airlines still carry other smelly cargo like cheese, or fermented liquids such as champagne. Herring haters say that if a can of herring is punctured, all the passengers suffer from the foul odor.

Fermented herring must age several months before it is sold. Suppose a newly built fish cannery were opened at the first of the year. If that factory produced 125,000 cans every month, and the canned fish had to be stored for five months before being sent to market, how many cans of herring could be shipped out of the factory during one calendar year?

Show your work here:

1

Whole Numbers
— Go Figure! —

British Cell Phone Recycling

A British researcher has invented a biodegradable cell phone case that, when buried, will grow into a sunflower. A sunflower seed is placed within the phone's cover, so that when the phone is discarded the cover may be removed and buried. An average of 118,000 cell phones are thrown away daily in Great Britain.

If all British cell phones begin using these biodegradable covers, how many sunflowers could be planted in a year within Great Britain via the recycled cell phone covers?

Show your work here:

2

Whole Numbers
— Go Figure! —

American Cell Phone Recycling

Since the average life of a cell phone is only eighteen months, about 130,000,000 cell phones are discarded in the United States each year. If those phones were recycled, a large amount of valuable and toxic material would be kept out of our landfills.

- Tons of arsenic, mercury, and lead would be eliminated from landfills.
- A large amount of gold, also used in cell phone manufacturing, would be saved.
- About 5,150 cell phones weigh one ton.
- Eight ounces of gold can be retrieved from one ton of old cell phones.
- In 2006, the price of gold was about $600 an ounce.

What is the value of one year's worth of America's old cell phones if they were all recycled? (Round all answers to the nearest whole number.)

Show your work here:

COMPUTE OR SIMPLIFY – USE A FORMULA – MAKE A PICTURE, DRAW A DIAGRAM – USE LOGICAL REASONING

MAKE A TABLE, LIST, OR CHART – GUESS AND CHECK – BRAINSTORM – FIND A PATTERN – WORK BACKWARDS

3

Whole Numbers
Go Figure!

A Cap an Hour

A Minnesota man has quite a cap collection. The ever-growing collection must be stored in several semi trailers at the Corn Palace in Mitchell, South Dakota. Started in 1970, the Minnesotan's collection has so many caps that he could wear a different cap *each hour* for nine years and six months.

How many caps does he have at this time? (Ignore leap years and use only whole numbers.)

Show your work here:

COMPUTE OR SIMPLIFY – USE A FORMULA – MAKE A PICTURE, DRAW A DIAGRAM – USE LOGICAL REASONING

MAKE A TABLE, LIST, OR CHART – GUESS AND CHECK – BRAINSTORM – FIND A PATTERN – WORK BACKWARDS

4

Whole Numbers
Go Figure!

Baseball Budgets

Critics of major league baseball point out that there is a great deal of difference between what teams can afford to pay their players each year. Take the example of the New York Yankees and the Tampa Bay Devil Rays, who happen to play in the same division.

- In 2005, the Yankees paid their 25-man roster $207,000,000. In 2006, the Yankees spent a little less.
- The difference between the '05 Yankee payroll and the '06 Yankee payroll was $3,000,000 *less* than the entire Tampa Bay payroll for 2006.
- The '06 Yankee payroll was 13 times that of the Devil Rays.

What was the payroll budgeted for each of these two teams in 2006?

Show your work here:

Left margin: COMPUTE OR SIMPLIFY – USE A FORMULA – MAKE A PICTURE, DRAW A DIAGRAM – USE LOGICAL REASONING

Right margin: MAKE A TABLE, LIST, OR CHART – GUESS AND CHECK – BRAINSTORM – FIND A PATTERN – WORK BACKWARDS

5

Whole Numbers

IP 723-1 • Copyright ©2007 by Incentive Publications, Inc., Nashville, TN.

"Pit"-iful Plea for Peace

A female follower of Buddhism from Japan buried herself in a 15-foot-deep pit in India in an effort to better the world. Disturbed by world events from war to natural disasters, the woman went without food and water for a full three days while she meditated in the pit.

If her meditation included counting numbers consecutively, one each second, how high would she have counted while she was in the pit?

Show your work here:

Left margin: COMPUTE OR SIMPLIFY – USE A FORMULA – MAKE A PICTURE, DRAW A DIAGRAM – USE LOGICAL REASONING

Right margin: MAKE A TABLE, LIST, OR CHART – GUESS AND CHECK – BRAINSTORM – FIND A PATTERN – WORK BACKWARDS

6

Whole Numbers

IP 723-1 • Copyright ©2007 by Incentive Publications, Inc., Nashville, TN.

Priceless 'Do

Political campaigns must be tough on the hair—at least in Great Britain. The wife of the British prime minister spent $490 each day during the almost month-long British election campaign in 2005. Unlike American presidential campaigns that last for the better part of a year, British campaigns are limited to four weeks.

How much did the prime minister's wife spend on hairstyles during that time?

Show your work here:

MAKE A TABLE, LIST, OR CHART – GUESS AND CHECK – BRAINSTORM – FIND A PATTERN – WORK BACKWARDS

COMPUTE OR SIMPLIFY – USE A FORMULA – MAKE A PICTURE, DRAW A DIAGRAM – USE LOGICAL REASONING

7

Whole Numbers
— Go Figure! —

Road Warrior

A northern California man has been identified as the person with the longest daily commute in the United States. The man drives 186 miles—one way—to work in San Jose, California. He works five days a week. In recognition of this distinction, the man will receive $10,000. His car gets 31 miles to the gallon.

With gas at about $3 a gallon, how long will the $10,000 prize pay for the gas used by the man's commute?

Show your work here:

MAKE A TABLE, LIST, OR CHART – GUESS AND CHECK – BRAINSTORM – FIND A PATTERN – WORK BACKWARDS

COMPUTE OR SIMPLIFY – USE A FORMULA – MAKE A PICTURE, DRAW A DIAGRAM – USE LOGICAL REASONING

8

Whole Numbers
— Go Figure! —

"Mr. Plastic Fantastic"

A California man holds the Guinness record for owning credit cards. He has 1,497 cards. He has been the record holder since 1971. The publishers of *The Guinness Book of World Records* have named him "Mr. Plastic Fantastic." Even though the combined credit limit from all his cards is $1,700,000, he uses only one card.

Based on the information given, what is the average credit limit on one of his cards? (Round your answer to the nearest whole dollar.)

Show your work here:

MAKE A TABLE, LIST, OR CHART — GUESS AND CHECK — BRAINSTORM — FIND A PATTERN — WORK BACKWARDS

COMPUTE OR SIMPLIFY — USE A FORMULA — MAKE A PICTURE, DRAW A DIAGRAM — USE LOGICAL REASONING

9

Whole Numbers
— Go Figure! —

Bummer Bus Ride

Students from a Nevada middle school took a four-hour bus ride to an amusement park in California only to find out that the park was closed for the day for which they had tickets. Apparently, the tour company responsible for organizing the trip had failed to call ahead to check on the park's operating schedule. The tour company agreed to completely pay for another trip to the park, and to refund the $50 each student had paid.

If four busses carrying 66 students each made the eight-hour round trip, how much money did the tour company lose through this mistake?

Show your work here:

MAKE A TABLE, LIST, OR CHART — GUESS AND CHECK — BRAINSTORM — FIND A PATTERN — WORK BACKWARDS

COMPUTE OR SIMPLIFY — USE A FORMULA — MAKE A PICTURE, DRAW A DIAGRAM — USE LOGICAL REASONING

10

Whole Numbers
— Go Figure! —

Gulf Stream Drift

A U.S. Navy jet crashed near Key West, Florida, on October 3, 2002. A piece of the tail section was found on a beach in Ireland some 4,900 miles northeast of the crash site on May 8, 2006. The Gulf Stream current apparently carried the wreckage to the distant beach.

How many miles did the tail section travel each day, on average, before it washed ashore in Ireland? (Round to the nearest whole number.)

Show your work here:

MAKE A TABLE, LIST, OR CHART – GUESS AND CHECK – BRAINSTORM – FIND A PATTERN – WORK BACKWARDS

COMPUTE OR SIMPLIFY – USE A FORMULA – MAKE A PICTURE, DRAW A DIAGRAM – USE LOGICAL REASONING

11

Whole Numbers
— Go Figure! —

Doggie De-gasser

A company in Cedar Rapids, Iowa, has manufactured a strap-on deodorizer of dog gas. Looking like a three-inch-wide thong that has a hole in it for the dog's tail, the invention is made from charcoal cloth designed to absorb the obnoxious odors that Fido might release. The product will be sold in packs of 40 for $20 a pack. One thong eliminates odor during one day of indoor use.

If a family has three dogs with serious gas problems during the month of August, how much money will the family spend to neutralize the doggie gas during that month?

Show your work here:

MAKE A TABLE, LIST, OR CHART – GUESS AND CHECK – BRAINSTORM – FIND A PATTERN – WORK BACKWARDS

COMPUTE OR SIMPLIFY – USE A FORMULA – MAKE A PICTURE, DRAW A DIAGRAM – USE LOGICAL REASONING

12

Whole Numbers
— Go Figure! —

The "Banana Dollar" Bill

At an auction of rare paper money in early 2006, an unusual piece of U.S. paper currency was sold for the second time in its existence. First printed in 1996, the bill has a banana sticker bearing the name of a fruit company embedded in the bill next to the picture of a famous American. Somehow the fruit sticker landed on this bill while it was in the middle of the printing process. The bill first sold for 505 times its face value in 2002. At the recent auction, it sold for $25,300 ($50 more than 2.5 times its selling price in 2002).

What is the actual face value of this bill?

Show your work here:

COMPUTE OR SIMPLIFY – USE A FORMULA – MAKE A PICTURE, DRAW A DIAGRAM – USE LOGICAL REASONING

MAKE A TABLE, LIST, OR CHART – GUESS AND CHECK – BRAINSTORM – FIND A PATTERN – WORK BACKWARDS

13

Algebraic Equations
Go Figure!

Slightly Overdue

An 85-year-old woman in Rotorua, New Zealand, won't have to pay her library fine. A book she borrowed from the local library in 1945 was found during a move. Based on the borrowing rules pasted inside the front cover of the book, the fine should have been over $6,000. However, the library simply asked for the privilege of displaying the book that was overdue for 61 years.

Based on the following pieces of information, what is the library's daily fine?

- The total fine was $6,679.80.
- The book was overdue for 61 years.
- For the first two weeks of the overdue period, there was a set fine per day.
- The second two-week overdue period doubled the fine per day.
- After four weeks, the fine per day was tripled.

Show your work here:

COMPUTE OR SIMPLIFY – USE A FORMULA – MAKE A PICTURE, DRAW A DIAGRAM – USE LOGICAL REASONING

MAKE A TABLE, LIST, OR CHART – GUESS AND CHECK – BRAINSTORM – FIND A PATTERN – WORK BACKWARDS

14

Algebraic Equations
Go Figure!

Tower Racers

A German man and an Austrian woman claimed first place in their respective divisions in the Empire State Building Tower Race, a race up 86 flights of stairs—1,576 steps in all.

- Between the first- and second-place finishers in the men's and women's divisions, the combined time of the top four racers was 2,705 seconds.

- The second-place men's finisher came in 17 seconds after the men's winner.

- The first-place woman's time was 64 seconds longer than the time of the men's winner.

- The second-place women's finisher took 84 seconds longer than the women's champion.

What was the time for each runner in minutes and seconds?

Show your work here:

MAKE A TABLE, LIST, OR CHART – GUESS AND CHECK – BRAINSTORM – FIND A PATTERN – WORK BACKWARDS

COMPUTE OR SIMPLIFY – USE A FORMULA – MAKE A PICTURE, DRAW A DIAGRAM – USE LOGICAL REASONING

15

Algebraic Equations
— Go Figure! —

Rattlesnake Roundup

Every March in Sweetwater, Texas, thousands of pounds of live Western diamondback rattlesnakes are collected in the Sweetwater Rattlesnake Roundup. The event draws spectators and rattlesnake handlers from across the nation. At the most recent roundup the first 2,000 pounds of live snakes brought in by a rattlesnake handler were valued at $5 per pound. Any snakes brought in beyond the first ton were priced at $4 a pound.

One contestant earned $4,100. Part of his catch was paid at the rate of $5 per pound, while the rest of it was paid at $4 per pound. If this rattlesnake wrangler's $5 per pound weight was 80 pounds less than the $4 per pound weight, what was the total weight of snakes that this contestant corralled?

Show your work here:

MAKE A TABLE, LIST, OR CHART – GUESS AND CHECK – BRAINSTORM – FIND A PATTERN – WORK BACKWARDS

COMPUTE OR SIMPLIFY – USE A FORMULA – MAKE A PICTURE, DRAW A DIAGRAM – USE LOGICAL REASONING

16

Algebraic Equations
— Go Figure! —

Salad Lovers' Feast

Twenty-seven members of a West Virginia diet club celebrated the combined loss of 500 pounds by devouring a very large salad. The salad took two hours to prepare and four hours to eat. In fact, the salad was mixed in a swimming pool and included 890 individual vegetables. There were six times as many carrots as heads of lettuce, and there were ten more cucumbers than heads of lettuce.

If a head of lettuce weighs two pounds, a carrot weighs four ounces, and a cucumber weighs one pound, how much did the total salad weigh?

Show your work here:

17

Algebraic Equations
— Go Figure! —

Pet Hotel

A pet hotel opened recently in Omaha, Nebraska. It features a color television and the opportunity for pampered pooches to phone their owners. Cats are pampered as well with special ice cream treats. Nightly lodging rates are $21 for small dogs, $26 for medium-sized dogs, $31 for large dogs, and $14 for cats. One night there were 31 guests.

- The guests included twice as many small dogs as medium dogs.
- Large dogs were the smallest number of animals in the hotel.
- There were seven times as many cats as there were large dogs.
- The hotel collected $598 in guest fees for the evening.

How many of each kind and size of pet stayed at the hotel that night?

Show your work here:

18

Algebraic Equations
— Go Figure! —

Up a Tree

A man in India left his wife after an argument and climbed up a tree to cool down. He hasn't moved back home since. He has continued to live in the tree among venomous snakes, and he says that he has found spiritual satisfaction. He comes down only to drink water from a nearby pond.

Solve this equation to determine how many years (Y) the man has lived in the tree.

$$Y + (3 \times 10) + 3 = 83$$

Show your work here:

COMPUTE OR SIMPLIFY – USE A FORMULA – MAKE A PICTURE, DRAW A DIAGRAM – USE LOGICAL REASONING

MAKE A TABLE, LIST, OR CHART – GUESS AND CHECK – BRAINSTORM – FIND A PATTERN – WORK BACKWARDS

19

Algebraic Equations
Go Figure!

Pawnbroking for Gas

Pawnbrokers lend money to people who need money right away. The borrower leaves a valuable item, such as a watch, with the broker (called *pawning* the item); the broker gives the borrower money; later, the borrower repays the money (plus interest) to the broker, who returns the item originally *pawned*.

With gasoline prices over $3 a gallon, some Americans have gone to pawnbrokers to borrow enough money to fill their tanks until their next payday. A certain pawnbroker charges 20% interest. Five people brought five separate items to this broker—a television, jewelry, a set of tools, a DVD player, and a PlayStation—in order to get money to buy gas.

- The total interest charged on the pawn of the set of tools was three times higher than the interest on the pawn of the television or the PlayStation.
- Interest on the pawn of the jewelry was two times the amount of the interest on the pawn of the television or PlayStation.
- The DVD's interest was $4 less than the interest on the television or PlayStation.

If the total interest the pawnbroker made on these five items was $156, how much money was borrowed on each item by each person who brought it to the pawnbroker?

Show your work here:

COMPUTE OR SIMPLIFY – USE A FORMULA – MAKE A PICTURE, DRAW A DIAGRAM – USE LOGICAL REASONING

MAKE A TABLE, LIST, OR CHART – GUESS AND CHECK – BRAINSTORM – FIND A PATTERN – WORK BACKWARDS

20

Algebraic Equations
Go Figure!

The Biggest Burger

A Clearfield, Pennsylvania, restaurant makes a 15-pound hamburger, the world's largest burger. It sells for $40, which is 16 times more than the restaurant's half-pound burger.

If a party of 30 people came in after a football game, each wishing to eat hamburgers, which would be the better value when ordering—one "world's largest burger" shared by the entire party, or a half-pound burger for each person? Explain your answer.

Show your work here:

COMPUTE OR SIMPLIFY – USE A FORMULA – MAKE A PICTURE, DRAW A DIAGRAM – USE LOGICAL REASONING

MAKE A TABLE, LIST, OR CHART – GUESS AND CHECK – BRAINSTORM – FIND A PATTERN – WORK BACKWARDS

21

Decimals
Go Figure!

Noah's Ark

A Dutchman is building a working replica of Noah's Ark in the Netherlands. It will be one-fifth the size of the ark as detailed in the book of Genesis in the Bible. The man estimates that at least 100,000 people will need to visit the ark if he is to break even on the project. His initial costs included $1,200,000 in land, labor, and materials to build the ark.

If the builder had to get an 8% simple-interest loan for one year to finance the project, how much will he have to charge each of the first 100,000 visitors to break even on the project?

Show your work here:

COMPUTE OR SIMPLIFY – USE A FORMULA – MAKE A PICTURE, DRAW A DIAGRAM – USE LOGICAL REASONING

MAKE A TABLE, LIST, OR CHART – GUESS AND CHECK – BRAINSTORM – FIND A PATTERN – WORK BACKWARDS

22

Decimals
Go Figure!

More Than a Bucket and Sponge

A car wash in Surrey, England, doesn't give just an ordinary wash. Using costly Brazilian waxes, purified water, and imported towels, the enterprise caters to famous entertainers and pro sports stars. The car wash owner charges 4,800 British pounds for his exclusive 61-stage wash.

If a British pound is worth $1.86, how much is a car wash in U.S. dollars?

Show your work here:

MAKE A TABLE, LIST, OR CHART — GUESS AND CHECK — BRAINSTORM — FIND A PATTERN — WORK BACKWARDS

COMPUTE OR SIMPLIFY — USE A FORMULA — MAKE A PICTURE, DRAW A DIAGRAM — USE LOGICAL REASONING

23

Decimals
Go Figure!

Big Fish

A man fishing in Lake Erie near Erie, Pennsylvania, speared that state's record carp while bow fishing. The fish was 49 inches long and weighed 54 pounds, 4 ounces.

To the nearest thousandth of a pound, how many pounds per inch is that?

Show your work here:

MAKE A TABLE, LIST, OR CHART — GUESS AND CHECK — BRAINSTORM — FIND A PATTERN — WORK BACKWARDS

COMPUTE OR SIMPLIFY — USE A FORMULA — MAKE A PICTURE, DRAW A DIAGRAM — USE LOGICAL REASONING

24

Decimals
Go Figure!

Marathon Toddler

A four-year-old Indian boy set a track record for his age when he ran an average of 5.7143 miles per hour for seven hours. He ran nonstop and would have continued to run, but doctors stopped him fearing exhaustion might set in.

How far did he run? (Round to the nearest whole number.)

Show your work here:

MAKE A TABLE, LIST, OR CHART – GUESS AND CHECK – BRAINSTORM – FIND A PATTERN – WORK BACKWARDS

COMPUTE OR SIMPLIFY – USE A FORMULA – MAKE A PICTURE, DRAW A DIAGRAM – USE LOGICAL REASONING

25

Decimals
Go Figure!

The Big Chill

A Briton set a record in May, 2006 when he swam 1.2 kilometers in the bone-chilling waters of a Norwegian glacial fjord. It took him 24 minutes to accomplish the swim.

Since a kilometer is .625 miles, how long would it have taken him (at his current rate) to swim one mile?

Show your work here:

MAKE A TABLE, LIST, OR CHART – GUESS AND CHECK – BRAINSTORM – FIND A PATTERN – WORK BACKWARDS

COMPUTE OR SIMPLIFY – USE A FORMULA – MAKE A PICTURE, DRAW A DIAGRAM – USE LOGICAL REASONING

26

Decimals
Go Figure!

Every Penny Counts

A Michigan woman, who paid all but $.01 of a $1,662.08 electric bill, had her power turned off by her electric company. The power was turned back on after the woman paid the penny owed. The elderly woman actually got assistance in paying the bill before the $.01 fiasco occurred. The Michigan Department of Human Services paid about half of the bill. Then the Salvation Army paid $430.67. The electric company had even helped her out by paying $430.66.

How much of the electric bill had the Department of Human Services actually paid?

Show your work here:

COMPUTE OR SIMPLIFY – USE A FORMULA – MAKE A PICTURE, DRAW A DIAGRAM – USE LOGICAL REASONING

MAKE A TABLE, LIST, OR CHART – GUESS AND CHECK – BRAINSTORM – FIND A PATTERN – WORK BACKWARDS

27

Decimals
Go Figure!

Speed

An important business executive in Italy was caught speeding in northern Italy. He was testing his brand new Porsche sports car. He was clocked at 311 kilometers an hour and fined 357 Euros.

If a kilometer is .625 of a mile and a Euro was worth $1.25 at the time, how fast was the businessman man speeding in miles per hour, and what was his fine in dollars?

Show your work here:

COMPUTE OR SIMPLIFY – USE A FORMULA – MAKE A PICTURE, DRAW A DIAGRAM – USE LOGICAL REASONING

MAKE A TABLE, LIST, OR CHART – GUESS AND CHECK – BRAINSTORM – FIND A PATTERN – WORK BACKWARDS

28

Decimals
Go Figure!

Recycling Bonanza

A Utah man left his rented house of eight years filled with 70,000 empty beer cans. The landlord completed the big clean-up which included recycling the cans. He received $810 for all the cans.

If aluminum cans were being bought for $.60 a pound, how many pounds of cans were recycled? Approximately how many cans make up a pound?

Show your work here:

29

Decimals
Go Figure!

Message in a Bottle

On November 20, 2003, a fifth grader from Massachusetts placed a message in a plastic soft drink bottle and threw it into the Atlantic as part of a class project. Recently, the student received a letter from a man in Morocco (Northern Africa) who found the bottle message along the shore.

If the bottle traveled 4.61 miles each day of its 3,500-mile trip, on what day did it arrive on the Moroccan coast?

Show your work here:

30

Decimals
Go Figure!

The "Black Widow" of Gorgers

A 100-pound woman won an eating contest in New York City when she put away 26 grilled cheese sandwiches in 10 minutes. The same woman was also on record for eating 11 pounds of cheesecake in 9 minutes, 48 chicken tacos in 11 minutes, and 37 hot dogs with buns in 12 minutes. Since she regularly defeats men of much greater size, she has been dubbed the "Black Widow." In an 8-minute contest of eating hamburgers, she ate two in the first minute, six in the second, four in the third, and eight in the fourth minute.

How many burgers did she devour in the 8-minute time span?

Show your work here:

COMPUTE OR SIMPLIFY – USE A FORMULA – MAKE A PICTURE, DRAW A DIAGRAM – USE LOGICAL REASONING

MAKE A TABLE, LIST, OR CHART – GUESS AND CHECK – BRAINSTORM – FIND A PATTERN – WORK BACKWARDS

31

Number Patterns, Factors, Place Value
— Go Figure! —

IP 723-1 • Copyright ©2007 by Incentive Publications, Inc., Nashville, TN.

The Cats' Meow

A prison near Avenal, California, was overrun with stray cats. After an initial trapping, about 100 cats were still left roaming the penitentiary. Use the following information to solve the question:

- Assume half the cats are female.
- Assume the first litter occurs at six months.
- A female cat (queen) can breed at about six months of age.
- A queen can have two litters a year.
- For this problem, let's say the average litter is four kittens.
- Let's assume there is plenty of food to support the cats, and they remain healthy.

If left alone, how many cats would inhabit the prison in two years' time?

Show your work here:

COMPUTE OR SIMPLIFY – USE A FORMULA – MAKE A PICTURE, DRAW A DIAGRAM – USE LOGICAL REASONING

MAKE A TABLE, LIST, OR CHART – GUESS AND CHECK – BRAINSTORM – FIND A PATTERN – WORK BACKWARDS

32

Number Patterns, Factors, Place Value
— Go Figure! —

IP 723-1 • Copyright ©2007 by Incentive Publications, Inc., Nashville, TN.

The Shrinking Half-Ton Man

A South Dakota man, known several years earlier as the "Half-Ton Man" due to his 1,072-pound weight at the time, has dramatically changed. After having his stomach surgically reduced, he steadily lost weight over the next 18 months. During each of the first four months following the stomach surgery, he lost 30, 33, 36, and 30 pounds respectively.

With that rate of weight loss and a recent operation that removed 81 pounds of excess fat around his waist, what is his present weight?

Show your work here:

MAKE A TABLE, LIST, OR CHART – USE LOGICAL REASONING

COMPUTE OR SIMPLIFY – USE A FORMULA – MAKE A PICTURE, DRAW A DIAGRAM – USE LOGICAL REASONING

GUESS AND CHECK – BRAINSTORM – FIND A PATTERN – WORK BACKWARDS

33

Number Patterns, Factors, Place Value

Go Figure!

The Tower of Debt

In 1981, the *national debt* (the difference between the amount of money the government brings in through taxes and the amount it spends) grew to $1 trillion for the first time. At that time President Ronald Reagan said it was like a stack of thousand-dollar bills many miles high. In 2006, the national debt rose to just about $9 trillion.

If a stack of ten million thousand-dollar bills is .67 mile high, how high is a stack of 1,000 thousand-dollar bills that equals $9 trillion?

Show your work here:

MAKE A TABLE, LIST, OR CHART – GUESS AND CHECK – BRAINSTORM – FIND A PATTERN – WORK BACKWARDS

COMPUTE OR SIMPLIFY – USE A FORMULA – MAKE A PICTURE, DRAW A DIAGRAM – USE LOGICAL REASONING

34

Number Patterns, Factors, Place Value

Go Figure!

Serpent Kissing

A snake charmer in Malaysia tried to set a world's record when he kissed a venomous 15-foot cobra a number of times in three minutes. The exact number of times that he kissed the snake on its head is a two-digit odd number which is the product of two prime numbers. One of the factors is a single-digit prime number while the other is a double-digit prime factor. The sum of all the digits of the factors is 11 while the sum of the digits of the actual product is 6.

What is the number of the times that the man kissed the cobra in three minutes?

Show your work here:

35

Number Patterns, Factors, Place Value
— Go Figure! —

IP 723-1 • Copyright ©2007 by Incentive Publications, Inc., Nashville, TN.

Odds-Defying Birthdays

A Minnesota family has three children (ages 8 years, 1 year, and 11 months) who, strangely enough, share the exact same birthday. The date occurs in a month with 30 days. In a normal, non-leap year, the actual day of the year (a number up to 365) has 12 factors, and its digits add up to 15. When ordered from largest to smallest, *differences between the factors* are 48, 16, 8, 8, 4, 4, 2, 2, 1, 1, and 1.

What is the month and date of the children's birthday?

Show your work here:

36

Number Patterns, Factors, Place Value
— Go Figure! —

IP 723-1 • Copyright ©2007 by Incentive Publications, Inc., Nashville, TN.

Nonagenarian Driver's Ed

A Connecticut driving instructor is unusual in the sense that he specializes in refresher courses for drivers over 60. His age is also unique. The number that equals his age has only two factors—both of them prime, and one is over 30. The two digits of his age add up to 12. Both digits are multiples of three.

How old is this driving teacher?

Show your work here:

COMPUTE OR SIMPLIFY – USE A FORMULA – MAKE A PICTURE, DRAW A DIAGRAM – USE LOGICAL REASONING

MAKE A TABLE, LIST, OR CHART – GUESS AND CHECK – BRAINSTORM – FIND A PATTERN – WORK BACKWARDS

37

Number Patterns, Factors, Place Value
— Go Figure! —

IP 723-1 • Copyright ©2007 by Incentive Publications, Inc., Nashville, TN.

Too Much Pork??

"Pork," or wasteful spending by the government, included $\$2.9 \times 10^{10}$ in 2005 helping to build a total "national debt" (money that the government owes) of $\$8 \times 10^{12}$. Some of the wasted spending went to the following: $\$1.3 \times 10^{7}$ to help fund the "World Toilet Summit"; $\$5 \times 10^{5}$ for the Arctic Winter Games; and another $\$5 \times 10^{5}$ for the Teapot Museum in North Carolina.

Use your understanding of scientific notation to give the actual dollar amounts for each item in the problem.

Show your work here:

COMPUTE OR SIMPLIFY – USE A FORMULA – MAKE A PICTURE, DRAW A DIAGRAM – USE LOGICAL REASONING

MAKE A TABLE, LIST, OR CHART – GUESS AND CHECK – BRAINSTORM – FIND A PATTERN – WORK BACKWARDS

38

Number Patterns, Factors, Place Value
— Go Figure! —

IP 723-1 • Copyright ©2007 by Incentive Publications, Inc., Nashville, TN.

Wrong Number

A man in Malaysia was billed 806,400,000,000,000 ringgit ($2,180,000,000) by his deceased father's phone company for calls supposedly made after his father's death. The man had disconnected the phone after his father passed away. The company said it would investigate the case.

Write each monetary amount in scientific notation.

Show your work here:

COMPUTE OR SIMPLIFY – USE A FORMULA – MAKE A PICTURE, DRAW A DIAGRAM – USE LOGICAL REASONING

MAKE A TABLE, LIST, OR CHART – GUESS AND CHECK – BRAINSTORM – FIND A PATTERN – WORK BACKWARDS

39

Number Patterns, Factors, Place Value

Go Figure!

The Oldest Soccer Ball

History's oldest known soccer ball left its museum home in Great Britain during the summer of 2006 and traveled to the World Cup in Germany. The 450-year-old ball is made of a pig's bladder wrapped in deer leather.

Using only squared numbers from 1 to 11, give one combination of squared numbers (using each square no more than once) that adds up to 450.

Show your work here:

COMPUTE OR SIMPLIFY – USE A FORMULA – MAKE A PICTURE, DRAW A DIAGRAM – USE LOGICAL REASONING

MAKE A TABLE, LIST, OR CHART – GUESS AND CHECK – BRAINSTORM – FIND A PATTERN – WORK BACKWARDS

40

Number Patterns, Factors, Place Value

Go Figure!

Cracking the Code

The Da Vinci Code is a very popular book and movie. It was also the center of a lawsuit in Great Britain when the author of one book charged the author of The Da Vinci Code, Dan Brown, with plagiarizing his ideas. In early 2006, a British judge ruled that Brown had not stolen ideas about his book from the other author and therefore had not plagiarized it. In his 73-page ruling, the judge placed a code of his own within the text of his decision. Just as in Brown's book, the code was based on the historical Fibonacci sequence—1, 1, 2, 3, 5, 8, 13, 21 . . . The pattern is formed by adding the two previous numbers to get the next number in the sequence.

Use the Fibonacci sequence to decode the secret message placed in these paragraphs. (For the purpose of this problem, once you reach 21 in the Fibonacci sequence, go back to 1.)

Show your work here:

COMPUTE OR SIMPLIFY – USE A FORMULA – MAKE A PICTURE, DRAW A DIAGRAM – MAKE A PICTURE, DRAW A DIAGRAM – USE LOGICAL REASONING

MAKE A TABLE, LIST, OR CHART – GUESS AND CHECK – BRAINSTORM – FIND A PATTERN – WORK BACKWARDS

41

Number Patterns, Factors, Place Value
— Go Figure! —

The French Spider-Man

Alain Robert, a French skyscraper climber, has climbed more than 70 of the world's tallest buildings, including the Empire State Building and Eiffel Tower. He uses no ropes or special climbing gear, only his hands and feet.

Recently, he climbed a Paris office building in 13 stages, pausing to apply chalk at the end of each stage. He climbed the building using a particular repeating pattern of progress. The first five stages included the following number of stories in each stage of the climb: 1, 5, 3, 2, 6. The time taken for the first six stages was as follows: 2 minutes, 4 minutes, 3 minutes, 2 minutes, 5 minutes, and 3 minutes.

How many stories high was the building Robert climbed, and how long did it take him to climb it?

Show your work here:

COMPUTE OR SIMPLIFY – USE A FORMULA – MAKE A PICTURE, DRAW A DIAGRAM – USE LOGICAL REASONING

MAKE A TABLE, LIST, OR CHART – GUESS AND CHECK – BRAINSTORM – FIND A PATTERN – WORK BACKWARDS

42

Number Patterns, Factors, Place Value
— Go Figure! —

Flavor Au Jour

A doctor from Yale University has proposed a different diet based on eating one general flavor of foods per day. The doctor says that eating many flavors at once requires different sensors in the body to register that they are full. This leads to overeating. He claims that eating various recipes each day based upon a single main flavor will limit the number of body sensors needing to be filled.

Charlie was about to start this new diet. He laid out his calendar so six flavors would rotate through the month, one per day. In no specific order, they were melon, peach, orange, apple, strawberry, and pineapple. The first day of the month was a Sunday, and Charlie decided he would start with apple-flavored dishes. On the first Tuesday of the month he would enjoy pineapple flavor; the second Tuesday, orange; the third Tuesday, strawberry; the fourth Tuesday, melon.

If Charlie's birthday is on the 20th, what flavor will he have on his special day?

Show your work here:

COMPUTE OR SIMPLIFY – USE A FORMULA – MAKE A PICTURE, DRAW A DIAGRAM – USE LOGICAL REASONING

MAKE A TABLE, LIST, OR CHART – GUESS AND CHECK – BRAINSTORM – FIND A PATTERN – WORK BACKWARDS

43

Number Patterns, Factors, Place Value
Go Figure!

Pudgy Puss Cat

Recently it was reported that one of the fattest cats in the world weighs in at a whopping 33 pounds. He eats on a very organized schedule made up of three meals a day. Each meal consists of a number of 5.5-ounce cans of cat food. His Sunday schedule is eight cans of tuna cat food for breakfast, seven cans of turkey cat food for lunch, and three cans of chicken cat food for dinner. On Monday he eats seven cans of tuna for breakfast, six cans of turkey for lunch, and five cans of chicken for supper. On Tuesday the schedule calls for six cans of tuna for breakfast, five cans of turkey for lunch, and seven cans of chicken for supper.

Continuing this schedule, how many cans of each cat food will the cat eat on Saturday? Rounded to the nearest pound, how many pounds of food does it eat daily?

Show your work here:

COMPUTE OR SIMPLIFY – USE A FORMULA – MAKE A PICTURE, DRAW A DIAGRAM – USE LOGICAL REASONING

MAKE A TABLE, LIST, OR CHART – GUESS AND CHECK – BRAINSTORM – FIND A PATTERN – WORK BACKWARDS

44

Number Patterns, Factors, Place Value
Go Figure!

Wasp Eater

A 30-year-old Chinese man has established quite a reputation. Using only a plastic bag, a bamboo stick, and some smoke, he removes wasps' nests. His only requested payment is to take the nest home, so he can eat fried wasps! The man started the year by removing one nest each day on January 2, 5, 14, 16, 20, and 21.

If he continues at this pace, how many nests will he have removed by the end of June?

Show your work here:

COMPUTE OR SIMPLIFY — USE A FORMULA — MAKE A PICTURE, DRAW A DIAGRAM — USE LOGICAL REASONING

MAKE A TABLE, LIST, OR CHART — GUESS AND CHECK — BRAINSTORM — FIND A PATTERN — WORK BACKWARDS

45

Number Patterns, Factors, Place Value
— Go Figure! —

That's Why They're Called "Grunts"

Combat Marines in Iraq have a logical reason to be nicknamed "Grunts." They carry some 74 pounds of specialized equipment on them. Each of the 20 pieces of equipment weighs from $\frac{1}{10}$ of a pound (ear plugs) to 19 pounds (chest- and back-body armor in a body vest).

Just six of the pieces make up most of the weight. The chest- and back-body armor weighs 5 pounds more than the ammunition each soldier carries with him. An assortment of grenades weighs 1 pound more than the weight of the side-body armor. A hydration system with water is 1 pound less than the side-body armor. The M-16 rifle weighs $\frac{1}{7}$ of the combined weight of these six objects. Protective side-body armor weighs $\frac{1}{9}$ of the combined weight of these six pieces.

If the combined weight of these six pieces is 85% of the total weight of equipment that a Marine carries with him, what is the exact weight of each of these six pieces of equipment?

Show your work here:

COMPUTE OR SIMPLIFY — USE A FORMULA — MAKE A PICTURE, DRAW A DIAGRAM — USE LOGICAL REASONING

MAKE A TABLE, LIST, OR CHART — GUESS AND CHECK — BRAINSTORM — FIND A PATTERN — WORK BACKWARDS

46

Fractions and Percentages
— Go Figure! —

Lodging by the Pound

A hotel in northern Germany is renting rooms by the weight of its guests. The owner of the hotel, impressed by how much weight a regular guest had lost in a year's time, has started to charge guests rates based on their weight. He wants Germans to become more health conscious.

One group of eight guests included two separate families—the Henke family and the Schmidt family—renting one room each. The total bill for this two-family group was based on a flat rate of $.28 per pound.

- In the Henke family, husband Gunnar's weight was responsible for $\frac{1}{4}$ of the group's bill.
- Wife Helga Henke's weight was $\frac{1}{7}$ of the bill.
- Hans Schmidt's weight made up $\frac{1}{5}$ of the total weight while the weight of his wife, Heidi Schmidt, was $\frac{1}{8}$ of the total.
- Among the children, Fritz Henke's weight was $\frac{1}{12}$ of the total; the weight of Peter Schmidt was $\frac{1}{10}$ of the total; Ulla Henke's portion of the bill was $12.60; and Marie Schmidt was seven pounds less than Ulla.
- The combined weight of the two young girls was one pound less than 10% of the total weight.

How much did each family member weigh? What was the total bill?

Show your work here:

Fractions and Percentages
Go Figure!

IP 723-1 • Copyright ©2007 by Incentive Publications, Inc., Nashville, TN.

COMPUTE OR SIMPLIFY – USE A FORMULA – MAKE A PICTURE, DRAW A DIAGRAM – USE LOGICAL REASONING

MAKE A TABLE, LIST, OR CHART – GUESS AND CHECK – BRAINSTORM – FIND A PATTERN – WORK BACKWARDS

"Plop, Plop, Fizz, Fizz" Buffet

To celebrate the 75th anniversary of the introduction of the antacid tablet Alka-Seltzer, its maker, Bayer AG of Germany, served a Guinness record-setting buffet in Las Vegas. There were 40 soups and two-and-a-half times as many salads. There were one-and-a-half times as many desserts as salads. Finally, there were 550% more main dishes than soups.

How many dishes of each course were served, and what was the grand total of the number of dishes for this buffet?

Show your work here:

Fractions and Percentages
Go Figure!

IP 723-1 • Copyright ©2007 by Incentive Publications, Inc., Nashville, TN.

COMPUTE OR SIMPLIFY – USE A FORMULA – MAKE A PICTURE, DRAW A DIAGRAM – USE LOGICAL REASONING

MAKE A TABLE, LIST, OR CHART – GUESS AND CHECK – BRAINSTORM – FIND A PATTERN – WORK BACKWARDS

Nauseating Ice

A seventh-grade Florida girl conducted a revealing science project. Using a college's laboratory, she compared the levels of bacteria found in the ice of various fast food restaurants with the bacteria levels in the toilet water of the same restaurants. In most cases the toilet water was cleaner than the ice found in soft drink dispensing machines. In $\frac{3}{5}$ of samples taken from the ice, *E. coli* bacteria were found.

Using this information, if one of these fast food restaurants served 4,255 iced drinks in a day's time, how many would have traces of the *E. coli* bacteria?

Show your work here:

COMPUTE OR SIMPLIFY – USE A FORMULA – MAKE A PICTURE, DRAW A DIAGRAM – USE LOGICAL REASONING

MAKE A TABLE, LIST, OR CHART – GUESS AND CHECK – BRAINSTORM – FIND A PATTERN – WORK BACKWARDS

49

Fractions and Percentages
— Go Figure! —

Where in the World?

According to a 2006 poll conducted for the National Geographic Society, many young Americans, ages 18–24, know very little about geography—whether asked about the United States or the world. Below are findings from the survey. They are listed randomly.

a. $\frac{1}{3}$ of those who answered couldn't locate Louisiana on a map.

b. 48% couldn't find Mississippi.

c. Less than 3 in 10 thought world news was important.

d. 14% thought knowing a foreign language was important.

e. A little more than $\frac{2}{3}$ of those who answered didn't know a major earthquake had hit Pakistan in October 2005.

f. 6 out of 10 couldn't find Iraq on a map of the Middle East.

g. 47% couldn't find India on a map of Asia.

h. 75% couldn't find Israel on a map of the Middle East.

i. Slightly more than $\frac{3}{5}$ didn't know the border between North and South Korea was the most heavily militarized border in the world (the one with the most weapons).

j. $\frac{3}{10}$ thought (incorrectly) that the U.S.-Mexico border was the most militarized.

Rank the findings beginning with the finding representing the smallest group (#1) to the finding representing the largest group (#10).

Show your work here:

50

Fractions and Percentages
— Go Figure! —

Road Kill Auction

For a number of years the state of New Hampshire Fish and Game Department earned several thousand dollars each year by auctioning wildlife killed along the Granite State's roadways. The "road kill," required to be in relatively good shape, was stored in a large freezer until the annual December auction.

During the most recent auction three different collections of species made up the vast majority of frozen wildlife up for bid. Each of these collections made up one-third of the combined total. There was a set of bobcats, foxes, and otters. There was a group of beavers and fishers (a weasel-like mammal). The final third was a large collection of black bears. Beavers made up 16.1% of the overall total. There were as many bobcats as beavers. There were four more foxes than otters. There were 16 fishers.

What was the *total* number of road kill in these three collections, and how many were there of each species?

Show your work here:

51

Fractions and Percentages
Go Figure!

IP 723-1 • Copyright ©2007 by Incentive Publications, Inc., Nashville, TN.

Town for Sale

The northern California town of Bridgeville was up for sale again. Consisting of a dozen houses, a café, and a post office, the town was originally bought on eBay by a finance executive in 2004 for $700,000. The executive has placed a minimum bid of $1.75 million on his town. He is getting questions from potential buyers from as far away as China and Germany.

If he sells the town for the minimum bid, by how many percent would he have increased his original investment?

Show your work here:

52

Fractions and Percentages
Go Figure!

IP 723-1 • Copyright ©2007 by Incentive Publications, Inc., Nashville, TN.

Meteorite Auction

A number of unusual rocks, most of which were meteorites, were recently sold at a natural history auction in New York City. Together, five unique pieces brought a large amount of money.

- A meteorite with gemstones in it brought 8% of the total.
- A small piece of the moon brought 5% of the total.
- A small piece of a 15-ton meteorite was 10% of the total.
- A piece of an asteroid weighing more than 300 pounds brought 60% of the total.
- The fifth piece, a space rock with a hole in it that was found in Africa, sold for $26,350.

For what did each of the first four rocks sell, and what was the total price of all five?

Show your work here:

COMPUTE OR SIMPLIFY – USE A FORMULA – MAKE A PICTURE, DRAW A DIAGRAM – USE LOGICAL REASONING

MAKE A TABLE, LIST, OR CHART – GUESS AND CHECK – BRAINSTORM – FIND A PATTERN – WORK BACKWARDS

53

Fractions and Percentages
Go Figure!

IP 723-1 • Copyright ©2007 by Incentive Publications, Inc., Nashville, TN.

Norwegian Crime Wave

For reasons unknown, every year during the five days before Easter Norwegians go on sort of a *crime wave*. During the five-day Easter holiday, Norwegians buy an abnormally high number of crime novels to read in their vacation cabins in the countryside. Television and radio networks broadcast special criminal mysteries during the Easter break. Ironically, Norway has one of the lowest crime rates in the world.

Supposedly, in all of Norway one year, a total of 2,260 crime novels were sold the five days before the Easter break. Then, on Monday of the Easter break 3,050 more crime books were sold, with the following numbers of criminal novels sold on each of the next four days of Easter week, respectively: 2,167; 1,233; 2,250; and 2,600.

What was the percentage increase in crime novels sold during the Easter holiday week as compared to the previous five days' sales of the same type of book?

Show your work here:

COMPUTE OR SIMPLIFY – USE A FORMULA – MAKE A PICTURE, DRAW A DIAGRAM – USE LOGICAL REASONING

MAKE A TABLE, LIST, OR CHART – GUESS AND CHECK – BRAINSTORM – FIND A PATTERN – WORK BACKWARDS

54

Fractions and Percentages
Go Figure!

IP 723-1 • Copyright ©2007 by Incentive Publications, Inc., Nashville, TN.

Pizza Air

The only pizza delivery service in Nome, Alaska, is very unique. Besides serving the residents of Nome, a commuter airline delivers the pizzeria's food for free to numerous Eskimo villages in northwestern Alaska who otherwise wouldn't have delivery pizza.

A recent order was being readied to go out on the next flight. Five types of pizza were being shipped—reindeer sausage and onion; Polynesian chicken and green peppers; pepperoni, reindeer sausage, and bacon; green peppers, tomatoes, and onions; bacon and tomatoes. Sets of toppings had to be placed on 140 pizzas. Chicken topped $\frac{5}{28}$ of the pizzas; 59 pizzas were to have reindeer sausage; 40% of the pizzas were to have tomatoes; 34 pizzas were to have bacon; 10% of the pizzas were to have pepperoni.

How many of the five types of pizza were to be made? How many sets of toppings had to be prepared?

Show your work here:

Fractions and Percentages
Go Figure!

IP 723-1 • Copyright ©2007 by Incentive Publications, Inc., Nashville, TN.

Cliff Diving Auto

A Missouri man, frustrated with the condition of his used car, has decided upon a unique way of regaining the money he has invested in its repair. After sinking $1,800 into fixing the engine, $300 into new tires, and $500 in general repairs, the man got the idea to auction his car on eBay—in a way. He is auctioning the rights of any business to place its name and logo on his car before he sends the car hurtling off a 150-foot cliff. The winning bid will get a video of the car diving to its end for advertising purposes. The man believes if he gets 150% more in a bid than what he spent on total repairs, he will then have made 325% more than what his car would have brought had he simply sold it outright.

How much is he hoping to get, and how much would he have received if he had sold it in a normal fashion?

Show your work here:

Fractions and Percentages
Go Figure!

IP 723-1 • Copyright ©2007 by Incentive Publications, Inc., Nashville, TN.

Picky, Picky, Picky

According to the National Dental Survey, 60% of Great Britain's population picks their teeth with a variety of objects including: screwdrivers, earrings, scissors, needles, knives, and forks. Another 23% said they leave food stuck between their teeth (which risks gum disease and bad breath).

With a total population of about 60,000,000, about how many Britons are teeth pickers? How many leave food stuck in their teeth?

Show your work here:

COMPUTE OR SIMPLIFY – USE A FORMULA – MAKE A PICTURE, DRAW A DIAGRAM – USE LOGICAL REASONING

MAKE A TABLE, LIST, OR CHART – GUESS AND CHECK – BRAINSTORM – FIND A PATTERN – WORK BACKWARDS

57

Fractions and Percentages

The Owl Record

A woman in Leeds, Maine, has recently achieved a first-ever record in *The Guinness Book of World Records*. She has in her possession 18,055 separate items of owl memorabilia. Having bought most of the items at a sale a few years ago, she has everything from owl towels to a blue toilet seat adorned with a painting of a great horned owl.

One room of her collection supposedly contains only five types of items: owl necklaces, owl statues, owl wind chimes, owl greeting cards, and plush owl dolls. For every 45 items in the room, there are 10 necklaces, 12 statues, 4 wind chimes, 5 greeting cards and 14 dolls. There are a total of 48 wind chimes in this room.

How many owl necklaces, statues, greeting cards, and dolls are in this room? How many total items are in the room?

Show your work here:

COMPUTE OR SIMPLIFY – USE A FORMULA – MAKE A PICTURE, DRAW A DIAGRAM – USE LOGICAL REASONING

MAKE A TABLE, LIST, OR CHART – GUESS AND CHECK – BRAINSTORM – FIND A PATTERN – WORK BACKWARDS

58

Ratio and Proportion

Taking a Hike

A 410-pound man left San Diego, California, on a walk across America in order to lose his excess weight. His hike began in mid-April 2005. By mid-January 2006, he had walked about 2,000 miles, reaching Terre Haute, Indiana, weighing 318 pounds. In a nationally televised interview at that point he said that he was walking 7 hours a day, averaging 3 miles an hour. He had 800 miles to go to reach his goal of New York City.

If he maintained his rate of weight loss, speed, and time devoted to walking, approximately when would he reach New York City and how much would he weigh when he arrived?

Show your work here:

59

Ratio and Proportion
— Go Figure! —

Forehead Billboard

A Belgian student sold the rights to his forehead, and those of the guests who would attend his twentieth birthday party, in order to fund the party. A marketing company agreed to pay $2,800 to throw the party as long as each partygoer would have the company's logo painted on his or her forehead for the evening. The student was thrilled because he thought at most he might get $250 for his idea and be able to invite 50 friends. Now, he thinks he could invite many more.

If he thought he could invite 50 friends originally, how many could he afford to invite now (if he actually had that many friends)?

Show your work here:

60

Ratio and Proportion
— Go Figure! —

Precious Metals

The rapidly rising price of industrial metals is driving some European thieves to unique measures. Besides stealing from construction sites and factories, some robbers are more desperate. In Great Britain, one gang has been stealing heavy iron manhole covers. In France, heads were sawed off a World War I statue.

- The price of one ton of aluminum equaled $\frac{4}{5}$ the price of one ton of zinc.
- One ton zinc equaled $\frac{7}{15}$ the price of a ton of copper.
- The price of a ton of copper was $\frac{3}{4}$ the cost of a half ton of nickel.

Nickel was selling at $20,000 a ton. What was the price per ton of the other three metals?

Show your work here:

61

Ratio and Proportion

Glass Summit

A local Swiss tourism board is going to try to improve its area's tourist business by adding height to one of its mountain peaks. The Little Matterhorn currently has a natural altitude of 12,740 feet. The board's plan is to build a 394-foot-high regular square pyramid out of glass and place it on the summit, so the official altitude of the mountain would be over 13,000 feet. The length of one side of the pyramid's base will be 294 feet. What will be the volume of this glass pyramid?

Show your work here:

62

Geometric Figures and Area

The Biggest Wheel

The world's tallest Ferris wheel has opened in southern China. It is 525 feet in diameter, making it 82 feet wider than the previous largest Ferris wheel, the London Eye in Great Britain. The new record holder takes 30 minutes to make one rotation.

If the London Eye rotated at the same rate of speed, how long would it take to make one rotation?

Show your work here:

MAKE A TABLE, LIST, OR CHART – GUESS AND CHECK – BRAINSTORM – FIND A PATTERN – WORK BACKWARDS

COMPUTE OR SIMPLIFY – USE A FORMULA – MAKE A PICTURE, DRAW A DIAGRAM – USE LOGICAL REASONING

63

Geometric Figures and Area
— Go Figure! —

Car of the Future?

A British inventor has created an automobile that he claims is the world's most fuel efficient vehicle. Supposedly it gets 8,000 miles to a gallon of gasoline. He believes one physical characteristic of the car is chiefly responsible for its high gas mileage.

What do you believe is the characteristic of this unique vehicle that gives it tremendous gas mileage? As part of your brainstorming, draw a sketch of what you think it looks like including its dimensions for length and width.

Show your work here:

MAKE A TABLE, LIST, OR CHART – GUESS AND CHECK – BRAINSTORM – FIND A PATTERN – WORK BACKWARDS

COMPUTE OR SIMPLIFY – USE A FORMULA – MAKE A PICTURE, DRAW A DIAGRAM – USE LOGICAL REASONING

64

Geometric Figures and Area
— Go Figure! —

Mega Pizzas

Two American pizzerias are contending for the Guinness record for largest pizza. These are not one time pizzas made just for the sake of a record—they are routinely available from the menu. A pizza shop in Iowa has a round pizza that is 4 feet in diameter. A Pennsylvania pizzeria bakes a rectangular pizza measuring 3.5 feet by 4 feet.

Which pizza shop has the largest menu pizza?

Show your work here:

COMPUTE OR SIMPLIFY – USE A FORMULA – MAKE A PICTURE, DRAW A DIAGRAM – USE LOGICAL REASONING

MAKE A TABLE, LIST, OR CHART – GUESS AND CHECK – BRAINSTORM – FIND A PATTERN – WORK BACKWARDS

65

Geometric Figures and Area
— Go Figure! —

Mega Pizzas II

One 48″ round pizza from the Iowa pizzeria requires ten pounds of dough, 48 ounces of sauce, and five pounds of cheese. The shop also offers 12″, 16″, and 24″ round pizzas.

Based on the ingredient amounts for the 48″ pizza, how much of each main ingredient is used for each of the three smaller sizes of pizza?

Show your work here:

COMPUTE OR SIMPLIFY – USE A FORMULA – MAKE A PICTURE, DRAW A DIAGRAM – USE LOGICAL REASONING

MAKE A TABLE, LIST, OR CHART – GUESS AND CHECK – BRAINSTORM – FIND A PATTERN – WORK BACKWARDS

66

Geometric Figures and Area
— Go Figure! —

Real Lemons

MAKE A TABLE, LIST, OR CHART – GUESS AND CHECK – BRAINSTORM – FIND A PATTERN – WORK BACKWARDS

COMPUTE OR SIMPLIFY – USE A FORMULA – MAKE A PICTURE, DRAW A DIAGRAM – USE LOGICAL REASONING

In a small village on the island of Cyprus in the Mediterranean Sea the people have been shocked by the large lemons that have grown on their trees. Some of the lemons have a circumference of 25.12 inches.

If an average lemon has a diameter of $2\frac{1}{2}$ inches, how many times larger is a lemon being grown by these Cypriot villagers? Give your answer as a mixed number fraction.

Show your work here:

Concrete House

MAKE A TABLE, LIST, OR CHART – GUESS AND CHECK – BRAINSTORM – FIND A PATTERN – WORK BACKWARDS

COMPUTE OR SIMPLIFY – USE A FORMULA – MAKE A PICTURE, DRAW A DIAGRAM – USE LOGICAL REASONING

A man in Maine has built his house out of concrete instead of wood. The basement, the foot-thick exterior walls, the floors, windowsills, and even the countertops are made of concrete. The house is 2,300 square feet in size.

Suppose this house's area includes a 25-foot-square unheated garage. Also suppose that an average wooden house costs $100 per *heated* square foot and $75 per *unheated* square foot to build. The man who built the concrete house said that it cost 15% more to build than a wooden frame house of the same size.

How much did it cost to build the concrete house using the figures given?

Show your work here:

The Largest Slice

The largest slice of pizza sold in a New York City pizzeria is 16″ long on each side and 10″ wide at the crust.

If the slice were an exact triangle, what would be the area of this slice of pizza in square inches? (Round all calculations to the nearest tenth of an inch.)

Show your work here:

69

Geometric Figures and Area
Go Figure!

Putting the Squeeze on Florida

With every passing year, Florida experiences greater problems with a new invasive reptile species from Asia—the Burmese python. With a body that can grow up to 25 feet long and weigh 300 pounds, there are few, if any, natural predators to control it in the Sunshine State. That may very well include alligators.

The Burmese python can devour prey up to three times its own circumference, as its jaw bones can separate and its skin stretch to accommodate a large meal that may keep it happily fed for a month or more. A 13-foot Burmese python was found dead in the Everglades—its body ruptured with a 6-foot alligator sticking out of the snake's burst abdomen. Apparently the conquered gator was too big for the python to safely eat.

If the snake's diameter was 10 inches, the circumference of the gator had to have been larger than what size?

Show your work here:

70

Geometric Figures and Area
Go Figure!

Road Kill Gourmet

A 66-year-old man from Cornwall, England, has been eating fresh road kill for over 30 years. He takes pride in "eating for free." He dines on everything from deer and rabbit to the more unusual bat, otter, hedgehog, weasel, and fox. He says that as long as he cooks the meat at a very high temperature for a long time he is satisfied that it is safe to eat.

If the man cooked a fresh road kill of fox at 210 degrees Celsius, what temperature was it according to the Fahrenheit scale?

Show your work here:

71

Measurement
Go Figure!

A Miraculous Fall

An Austrian man accidentally fell 130 feet out of a helicopter and landed without injury.

If his fall took 3 seconds, how fast (in miles per hour) was he traveling when he hit the ground? On what type of surface might he have landed in order not to sustain any injuries?

Show your work here:

72

Measurement
Go Figure!

The B.O. Bank

Police in the eastern Chinese city of Nanjing have opened that nation's first body odor bank. It is a facility that holds a collection of over 500 human body smells designed to be compared to the odors at crime scenes. Specially trained police dogs use the sample smells to help track criminals. The smells in the bank are good for three years if kept at a temperature of –18 degrees Celsius.

At what temperature Fahrenheit must the sample odors be stored?

Show your work here:

COMPUTE OR SIMPLIFY – USE A FORMULA – MAKE A PICTURE, DRAW A DIAGRAM – USE LOGICAL REASONING

MAKE A TABLE, LIST, OR CHART – GUESS AND CHECK – BRAINSTORM – FIND A PATTERN – WORK BACKWARDS

73

Measurement
Go Figure!

IP 723-1 • Copyright ©2007 by Incentive Publications, Inc., Nashville, TN.

Gone With the Wind?

A 19-year-old Missouri man survived being taken for a mind-numbing ride by a tornado. The winds, clocked at 150 mile per hour, tore him out of his house trailer and deposited him in a soft, grassy field some 1,307 feet ($\frac{1}{4}$ mile) away from the trailer. Officials from the National Weather Service used a GPS device to accurately measure how far the man was carried.

Given the distance and speed of the winds, how long did the man fly in the storm?

Show your work here:

COMPUTE OR SIMPLIFY – USE A FORMULA – MAKE A PICTURE, DRAW A DIAGRAM – USE LOGICAL REASONING

MAKE A TABLE, LIST, OR CHART – GUESS AND CHECK – BRAINSTORM – FIND A PATTERN – WORK BACKWARDS

74

Measurement
Go Figure!

IP 723-1 • Copyright ©2007 by Incentive Publications, Inc., Nashville, TN.

Beer Plumbing

At $7.50 per 12 ounces, beer in Norway is the most expensive beer in the world. So it came as a real shock to a woman in a western Norway town when she turned on the faucet in her apartment and realized that beer, instead of water, was pouring out of it. Apparently, a worker in a bar two floors beneath the apartment mistakenly connected a keg of beer to the building's plumbing.

If the woman drew out $1\frac{7}{8}$ gallons of beer from her tap before the misaligned plumbing was corrected, what was the value of the beer that came from her faucet?

Show your work here:

COMPUTE OR SIMPLIFY – USE A FORMULA – MAKE A PICTURE, DRAW A DIAGRAM – USE LOGICAL REASONING

MAKE A TABLE, LIST, OR CHART – GUESS AND CHECK – BRAINSTORM – FIND A PATTERN – WORK BACKWARDS

Raccoon Barbecue

Each mid-January in an eastern Arkansas town, politicians and political wanna-bes get together for a dinner of barbecued raccoon. The raccoon meat—which experts say "tastes like raccoon"—entirely fills a walk-in freezer in the local high school cafeteria that measures 3′ by 2′ by 5′.

If the meat comes in freezer boxes that measure 24″ by 12″ by 6″ and each box holds 24 pounds of meat, how many pounds of raccoon meat will be served at the dinner?

Show your work here:

COMPUTE OR SIMPLIFY – USE A FORMULA – MAKE A PICTURE, DRAW A DIAGRAM – USE LOGICAL REASONING

MAKE A TABLE, LIST, OR CHART – GUESS AND CHECK – BRAINSTORM – FIND A PATTERN – WORK BACKWARDS

The Biggest Pie Ever!

The folks in New Bremen, Ohio, decided to go for a Guinness record in November 2005. They were going to make the world's largest pie of any kind. They ended up making a 12-foot-wide pumpkin pie that had filling 6 inches deep. The entire pie weighed over 1 ton. In February 2006, Guinness officials recognized the pie as a record.

If the filling alone weighed 1 ton, how much did 1 cubic foot of the filling weigh?

Show your work here:

COMPUTE OR SIMPLIFY – USE A FORMULA – MAKE A PICTURE, DRAW A DIAGRAM – USE LOGICAL REASONING

MAKE A TABLE, LIST, OR CHART – GUESS AND CHECK – BRAINSTORM – FIND A PATTERN – WORK BACKWARDS

77

A Foul Flood

A village in southern Germany was flooded by liquid pig manure when a tank holding the fertilizer ruptured. The smelly contents, 63,000 gallons in all, covered much of the village two feet deep in wretched ooze.

If five gallons of manure weighs 29 pounds and one cubic foot of manure weighs 43.5 pounds, figure the total weight and volume of the manure. Draw a diagram of the tank (with dimensions) that could have held the full amount of stinky pig waste.

Show your work here:

COMPUTE OR SIMPLIFY – USE A FORMULA – MAKE A PICTURE, DRAW A DIAGRAM – USE LOGICAL REASONING

MAKE A TABLE, LIST, OR CHART – GUESS AND CHECK – BRAINSTORM – FIND A PATTERN – WORK BACKWARDS

78

The Astro Turf Car

In an effort to promote the use of biodiesel—a fuel made from recycled cooking oil—an Oregon man has covered his 1982 Volkswagen in green Astro turf. Except for the windows, front radiator grill and lights, the entire vehicle is covered in segments of the artificial grass that measure 15 inches by 15 inches.

If the entire metallic surface area of the Volkswagen is 90 square feet, how many complete turf sections were needed to cover it?

Show your work here:

MAKE A TABLE, LIST, OR CHART – GUESS AND CHECK – BRAINSTORM – FIND A PATTERN – WORK BACKWARDS

COMPUTE OR SIMPLIFY – USE A FORMULA – MAKE A PICTURE, DRAW A DIAGRAM – USE LOGICAL REASONING

79

Surface Area and Volume
— Go Figure! —

Lost Wallet Found

A Florida couple accidentally threw away the wife's wallet with the outgoing trash. The husband called the trash hauling company in time for the truck to unload its cargo of rubbish in a garbage transfer station. The company was able to give the husband one hour and several workers to look through 14 tons of garbage before other trucks would arrive to dump more garbage in the station. In the last remaining minutes of the search a worker found the wallet, safe and clean inside a plastic bag.

If seven pounds of garbage equal one cubic foot of garbage, draw a diagram that gives an accurate picture of the size of this pile of garbage.

Show your work here:

MAKE A TABLE, LIST, OR CHART – GUESS AND CHECK – BRAINSTORM – FIND A PATTERN – WORK BACKWARDS

COMPUTE OR SIMPLIFY – USE A FORMULA – MAKE A PICTURE, DRAW A DIAGRAM – USE LOGICAL REASONING

80

Surface Area and Volume
— Go Figure! —

Sewage Gusher

Workers trying to dislodge a grease clog in a sewage line in Charlotte, North Carolina, used a high pressure hose to blast through it. Unfortunately, it sent 3,000 gallons of sewage gushing like a mini geyser out of the toilet of a nearby home for almost an hour.

Calculate the depth of the sludge left in the house given the following information:

- 5 gallons of sewage weighs 29 pounds;
- 1 cubic foot of sewage weighs 43.5 pounds;
- The house is 35 feet long by 35 feet wide.

Show your work here:

COMPUTE OR SIMPLIFY – USE A FORMULA – MAKE A PICTURE, DRAW A DIAGRAM – USE LOGICAL REASONING

MAKE A TABLE, LIST, OR CHART – GUESS AND CHECK – BRAINSTORM – FIND A PATTERN – WORK BACKWARDS

81

Surface Area and Volume
— Go Figure!

Recorded on Ice

A Brazilian man, who makes a living by setting unusual records, broke his own record for being buried in ice. Standing in a clear, acrylic box with shaved ice up to his neck, the man lasted over 66 minutes. The stunt was held at a shopping mall.

The box was approximately 3 feet wide, 4.5 feet long, and 6 feet high. If the man took up $\frac{1}{3}$ of the volume of the box, and $\frac{2}{9}$ of the box's volume was just air, how many cubic feet of ice were placed in the box?

Show your work here:

COMPUTE OR SIMPLIFY – USE A FORMULA – MAKE A PICTURE, DRAW A DIAGRAM – USE LOGICAL REASONING

MAKE A TABLE, LIST, OR CHART – GUESS AND CHECK – BRAINSTORM – FIND A PATTERN – WORK BACKWARDS

82

Surface Area and Volume
— Go Figure!

The People Zoo

Four Australian men lived in a glass box in downtown Shanghai, China, in June 2006 for two weeks. The public was able to watch almost every aspect of the men's lives—eating, sleeping, and bathing—through the glass walls of the 13 foot by 50 foot by 8 foot room. Only the bathroom portion of the room had nontransparent glass to keep that area private. The room was set in a Shanghai mall with people able to watch activity within the glass walls from five sides. Only the floor was not made of glass.

How much viewable surface area was in this strange room?

Show your work here:

COMPUTE OR SIMPLIFY – USE A FORMULA – MAKE A PICTURE, DRAW A DIAGRAM – USE LOGICAL REASONING

MAKE A TABLE, LIST, OR CHART – GUESS AND CHECK – BRAINSTORM – FIND A PATTERN – WORK BACKWARDS

83

Surface Area and Volume

Go Figure!

Pig Games

Every year the city of Moscow, in Russia, holds a kind of pig "Olympics." A group of 12 piglets compete in three events—pig-racing, pig-swimming, and pig-ball where the little swine try to push a small soccer ball into a net with their snouts.

Assuming the pigs are of equal ability, what is the probability that any specific piglet will win at least one event?

Show your work here:

COMPUTE OR SIMPLIFY – USE A FORMULA – MAKE A PICTURE, DRAW A DIAGRAM – USE LOGICAL REASONING

MAKE A TABLE, LIST, OR CHART – GUESS AND CHECK – BRAINSTORM – FIND A PATTERN – WORK BACKWARDS

84

Probability

Go Figure!

Valued Felines

A village in China threw a fish banquet for 200 cats which rid their farmland of rats. Previously, the villagers had exterminated snakes in the area which led to the surge in the number of rats. The cats were bought and turned loose to control the rats.

If there were equal numbers of brown rats and black rats in the region and the cats consisted of the following color types—50 calico; 30 gray tigers; 30 yellow tabbies; 20 tuxedos (black and white); 40 all black; and 30 all gray—which color type cat had the highest probability of catching the first brown rat?

Show your work here:

COMPUTE OR SIMPLIFY — USE A FORMULA — MAKE A PICTURE, DRAW A DIAGRAM — USE LOGICAL REASONING

MAKE A TABLE, LIST, OR CHART — GUESS AND CHECK — BRAINSTORM — FIND A PATTERN — WORK BACKWARDS

85

Probability
Go Figure!

Sardine Ice Cream

An ice cream shop in Portugal opened for business with dozens of new and exotic flavors of ice cream. While customers were able to buy vanilla and chocolate, this Portuguese ice cream parlor certainly offered more. It introduced flavors such as sardine, cod, trout, tuna, shrimp, spaghetti, garlic, and orange liquor. At the grand opening a large tub of ice held a number of randomly placed individual serving boxes of the new flavors. There were 20 containers of trout flavor, 10 containers of shrimp flavor, 10 boxes of cod flavor, 30 of tuna flavor, 50 of sardine flavor, 40 of spaghetti flavor, 20 of garlic flavor, and 20 of orange liquor.

If someone reached in without looking and picked two boxes, what chance does the person have of selecting one box each of sardine and spaghetti flavored ice cream?

Show your work here:

COMPUTE OR SIMPLIFY — USE A FORMULA — MAKE A PICTURE, DRAW A DIAGRAM — USE LOGICAL REASONING

MAKE A TABLE, LIST, OR CHART — GUESS AND CHECK — BRAINSTORM — FIND A PATTERN — WORK BACKWARDS

86

Probability
Go Figure!

"Crash" the Mailman

A 39-year-old mailman in Croatia has turned to riding a bicycle after having his 33rd automobile wreck in 23 years. Since he turned 16, he has had at least one car accident each year; luckily, he has never been seriously hurt.

If the mailman has been driving for 23 years and 9 months, what would be the probability based on his driving record that he would have an accident next month (had he continued driving)?

Show your work here:

MAKE A TABLE, LIST, OR CHART – GUESS AND CHECK – BRAINSTORM – FIND A PATTERN – WORK BACKWARDS

COMPUTE OR SIMPLIFY – USE A FORMULA – MAKE A PICTURE, DRAW A DIAGRAM – USE LOGICAL REASONING

87

Probability
Go Figure!

Against All Odds

An Iowa man defied tremendous odds when he won three state lottery game jackpots totaling over $80,000 in one year. He won one game's grand prize twice. That game had 1 in 90,000 odds of winning. He won his third jackpot on a game in which the odds of winning were 1 in 120,000.

What odds did he overcome to win the three jackpots in three separate attempts?

Show your work here:

MAKE A TABLE, LIST, OR CHART – GUESS AND CHECK – BRAINSTORM – FIND A PATTERN – WORK BACKWARDS

COMPUTE OR SIMPLIFY – USE A FORMULA – MAKE A PICTURE, DRAW A DIAGRAM – USE LOGICAL REASONING

88

Probability
Go Figure!

Surprise Driver

Law enforcement officers in Tennessee were following an apparently drunken driver who nearly had five head-on collisions in a seven-mile chase before turning into a local home's driveway. They were shocked to find that the driver wasn't drunk at all—he was only seven years old! The four-foot-tall tyke said he was just ready to learn how to drive.

- The total number of law enforcement vehicles—local police, county sheriff, and state highway patrol—involved in the chase was less than 15.
- The number of local police cars was one more than the combined number of sheriff and highway patrol cars.
- The highway patrol had the least number of cars involved.

If the total number of all law enforcement vehicles involved is not a prime number, what was the exact number of each type in the chase?

Show your work here:

The Fugitive Heifer

A 1,200-pound cow escaped a meat packing plant near Great Falls, Montana, and proceeded to go on a seven-hour adventure. Its time on the run included:

- a standoff in a park with plant workers and animal control officers
- near-fatal encounters with an SUV, a semi tractor-trailer, and a railroad locomotive
- a desperate crossing of the frigid Missouri River
- temporary freedom gained by running through a fence
- a wild romp through a residential neighborhood

The heifer was nearly hit by the SUV before it tangled first with the locomotive and then with the semi-truck. It bolted through the fence before it ever came into the path of any vehicle, but that wasn't the first adventure in its getaway. The near-miss by the semi came right before the standoff in the park. When it was eventually tranquilized and caught, the heifer was covered with ice.

Give the exact order of the frantic cow's seven-hour misadventure.

Show your work here:

Dreaded Dress Code

In this problem similar to an actual case where a Kansas high school student was sent home because her jeans were torn in too many places, seven students attending Smalltown Middle School were sent to the principal's office one day with dress-code violations. Three violators were 13-year-olds and four were 12-year-olds. Three were sent to the principal for having multi-colored hair, while four were sent for having "holey" jeans. Tim, Jason, and Derek were all brought in on the same offense. Donna and Sheila had different violations. Robert, Ann, and Donna are the same age. Tim and Jason are not the same age.

All were to be sent home until appropriate dress/hair color was maintained. Which two 12-year-olds were sent home for having multi-colored hair?

Show your work here:

91

IP 723-1 • Copyright ©2007 by Incentive Publications, Inc., Nashville, TN.

Unlucky Friday the 17th!

Curve #17 at the bobsled track in Cesana, Italy, is the only curve on the track without a non-numerical nickname—for good reason. In Italy, the number 17 has "misfortune" written all over it, just as the number 13 has in America. Friday the 17th is considered by some Italians to be an omen of bad luck. Apparently, this superstition goes back to ancient times and Roman numerals. The numeral for 17—XVII—can be written in Latin as "VIXI," which translates to *"I lived"* (without the "e"), or in a more general translation, *"I'm dead."*

Use the logic from this situation to determine what number would be the equivalent to *"I lived"* if based upon the English language.

Show your work here:

92

IP 723-1 • Copyright ©2007 by Incentive Publications, Inc., Nashville, TN.

The Chicken Coop Jackpot

A Hungarian chicken farmer found a Stradivarius violin in the attic of his chicken coop right where his father had apparently placed it for safekeeping during World War II over 60 years before. Violins made by Antonio Stradivari, an Italian instrument maker, are rare and greatly valued. This one may be worth several million dollars.

One reason offered for the value of a Stradivarius is that the wood used in these violins was very dense—giving the violin fantastic tonal qualities—because of a period of ultra-cold weather in Europe during the "Little Ice Age." The Little Ice Age began 19.2 decades before Columbus sailed for America. It lasted five-and-a-half centuries. The ultra-cold period began 70 years after the midpoint of the "Little Ice Age," and, lasting for seven decades, was the longest, coldest stretch of this climatic period. During the last 15 years of this seven decades-long cold stretch, Antonio Stradivari used Alpine spruce that had grown extremely dense (because of the cold) to make instruments in his Golden Period. His Golden Period lasted for five years beyond the end of this very cold stretch.

What span of years was Antonio Stradivari's Golden Period?

Show your work here:

MAKE A TABLE, LIST, OR CHART – GUESS AND CHECK – BRAINSTORM – FIND A PATTERN – WORK BACKWARDS

COMPUTE OR SIMPLIFY – USE A FORMULA – MAKE A PICTURE, DRAW A DIAGRAM – USE LOGICAL REASONING

93

Land Diving

On Pentecost Island in the South Pacific, an ancient tribal ritual is aiding the island's tourist industry. "Land diving" originated 1,500 years ago. Native men build towers out of wood up to 100 feet tall, climb to certain heights on the tower, install a break-away extension, then wrap a freshly cut vine around their ankle and attach it to the extension. A dive to the earth is just long enough that, if all goes right, the upper part of the diver's body will just touch earth in a pit of loosened soil at the bottom of the tower at the conclusion of the fall.

Jumping starts with youngsters at lower heights and then progresses, with the most experienced jumpers diving 100 feet. On one particular day of land diving, five divers leapt from 20 feet, 40 feet, 60 feet, 80 feet, and 100 feet. Of these divers, Raiko jumped from a height more than twice as high as the beginning jumper. Solomon jumped after Raiko. Fargo jumped from half the distance of Solomon. Torres wasn't the first jumper. Dano jumped from a height one-fourth that of Solomon's.

What was the height of each jumper's dive?

Show your work here:

MAKE A TABLE, LIST, OR CHART – GUESS AND CHECK – BRAINSTORM – FIND A PATTERN – WORK BACKWARDS

COMPUTE OR SIMPLIFY – USE A FORMULA – MAKE A PICTURE, DRAW A DIAGRAM – USE LOGICAL REASONING

94

The Bogus Billions

U.S. customs agents in California caught a man trying to smuggle 250 counterfeit billion-dollar bills.

How many $10,000 bills should a person get in exchange for a billion-dollar bill?

Show your work here:

COMPUTE OR SIMPLIFY – USE A FORMULA – MAKE A PICTURE, DRAW A DIAGRAM – USE LOGICAL REASONING

MAKE A TABLE, LIST, OR CHART – GUESS AND CHECK – BRAINSTORM – FIND A PATTERN – WORK BACKWARDS

95

Mental Mazes
Go Figure!

IP 723-1 • Copyright ©2007 by Incentive Publications, Inc., Nashville, TN.

A Flowery Bargain

A Florida flower shop, estimated to be worth $100,000 by its owners, is going to be sold for a mere $100. If all goes as planned, the owners will happily leave the flower business behind, and the new owner will have purchased it for only $100. The new owner will not be a member of the previous owners' family.

Explain why *both* owner and buyer will be very satisfied with this deal.

Show your work here:

COMPUTE OR SIMPLIFY – USE A FORMULA – MAKE A PICTURE, DRAW A DIAGRAM – USE LOGICAL REASONING

MAKE A TABLE, LIST, OR CHART – GUESS AND CHECK – BRAINSTORM – FIND A PATTERN – WORK BACKWARDS

96

Mental Mazes
Go Figure!

IP 723-1 • Copyright ©2007 by Incentive Publications, Inc., Nashville, TN.